Dinosaurs

10 9 8 7 6 5 4 3 2 1

Library of Congress Cataloging in Publication Data

Dimond, Jasper.
  Dinosaurs.

  Summary: a package including a book of text
describing different dinosaurs and a set of
punch-out models of these ancient reptiles.
    1. Dinosaurs—Juvenile literature.   2. Dinosaurs—
Models—Juvenile literature. [1. Dinosaurs. 2. Toy
and movable books]   I. Title.
QE862.D5D49   1985   567.9'1   84–26418
ISBN 0-13-214628-2

Dinosaurs
by Jasper Dimond

Prentice-Hall · Englewood Cliffs, NJ

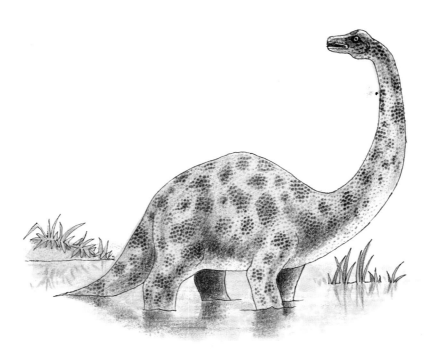

For Sally and Marcus

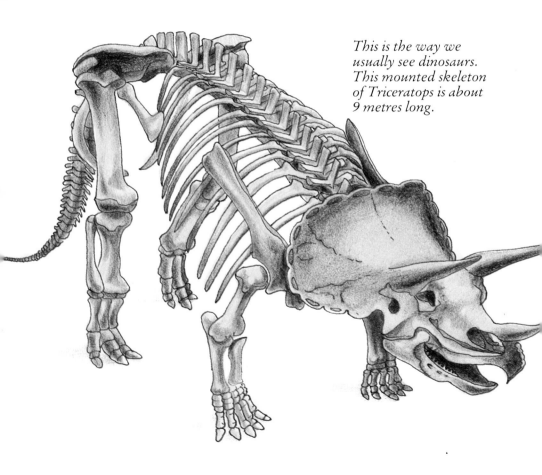

*This is the way we
usually see dinosaurs.
This mounted skeleton
of Triceratops is about
9 metres long.*

*I*f somebody asked you what a dinosaur was, what would your answer be? Perhaps you would say it was any kind of big animal which lived millions of years ago; or maybe you would decide it was one particular enormous prehistoric animal with a long neck, a long tail, and a brain the size of a peanut. Either answer would be wrong!

In fact, the word 'dinosaurs' describes a distinct group of animals, which was quite different from any other group, but which included a great variety of creatures.

Not all dinosaurs were big. Although some were the length of a Blue whale, others were no bigger than a starling; and they came in all sizes in between.

*B*ut of course there were some huge dinosaurs. One, found in 1972, in Colorado, is thought to have been more than 15 metres (50 feet) tall, and up to 30 metres long. Imagine an animal tall enough to look over a four-storey house, and as long as a Boeing 737 jet airliner! No wonder it was immediately nicknamed 'Supersaurus'.

'Supersaurus'

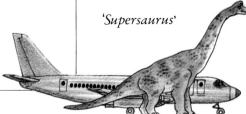

Again, most people think that all dinosaurs were meat-eaters (carnivores). But this is wrong too. You may be surprised to learn that perhaps as many as 95 in every 100 dinosaurs were plant-eaters (herbivores). The vast majority ate only plants and shrubs, and were probably quite placid unless attacked.

*Again*st all the evidence, a few people even believe that some dinosaurs may still be alive, hiding in remote parts of the world. But this is impossible. The world has been so thoroughly explored that no animal of any size could have remained undetected for so long. In any case, scientists have proved beyond a doubt that the last dinosaurs died

Iguanodons (iguana tooth), lived in the Early Cretaceous Period, about 136 million years ago. Some were as heavy as elephants, and they could rear up to 5 metres in height, although they sometimes walked on all fours. They roamed in herds in warm, swampy countryside, living on horse-tail plants and ferns. Their only weapons of defence were their spiked thumbs.

out about 65 million years ago – that is, well over 60 million years before people first appeared on the planet.

*M*any people have tried to find explanations for why dinosaurs disappeared, and scientists argue a lot about the different theories. One suggestion is that a gigantic rock from outer space hit the earth, and raised such a thick cloud of dust that the dinosaurs could not adapt quickly enough to the resulting change in the world's climate. Another is that egg-eaters evolved which were so successful that eventually there were no young dinosaurs left.

Other suggestions are that the dinosaurs grew too big, clumsy, and slow to escape their enemies, or that they all fell victim to some dangerous new disease.

But nobody really knows why they died out when they did, apparently all at about the same time, and probably no-one ever will.

*E*ven so, dinosaurs should not be considered a failure because they became extinct. They ruled the earth for 140 million

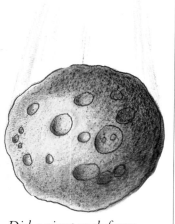

Did a giant rock from outer space hit the earth?

years, and from the remains that have been discovered so far, we know of up to 800 different kinds of dinosaur which lived at some time during this period. No other group of backboned animals, including humans, can claim anything like the same degree of success.

How we know about dinosaurs

*T*he natural world changes all the time, and has been doing so since the beginning of time itself. Even now, it is still changing, but so slowly that none of us lives long enough to notice any real difference to our surroundings (apart from man-made alterations). But these changes leave visible marks on the landscape, and, if you know how to 'read' the marks, they can reveal a great deal about the history of our planet. Indeed, all our knowledge of the far-distant past comes from a study of rocks, and of the fossils which we find in them.

The word 'fossil' is a Latin word which literally means 'something which has been dug up'. Nowadays, we normally use it to describe the remains of an animal or plant which has been buried in mud and rock and,

Did egg thieves kill off the dinosaurs?

over a period of thousands of years, has itself been turned into rock. Everything we know about dinosaurs comes from a study of these fossilised remains.

How fossils are made

When an animal dies, its body usually becomes food for other animals. Even the

Tyrannosaurus Rex (tyrant-lizard king) lived in the Late Cretaceous Period. The largest meat-eating animal that ever lived, it was up to 12 metres long, 5 metres tall, and 7 tonnes in weight. Its head alone measured 1.25 metres, and its jaws carried great saw-edged, curved teeth which were 15 centimetres long. It had enormously powerful hind legs, and great clawed feet. But its fore-limbs were tiny, with only two fingers on each hand.

bones are chewed up and scattered over a wide area. Anything that remains quickly decays and becomes part of the soil. But if an animal dies in the sea, by a river which floods, or near a swamp or lake, it stands a better chance of being preserved.

Gradually, its body sinks into the mud and its flesh rots away, leaving its bony skeleton complete. Time passes, and sand sinks through the water and covers the skeleton. As more and more sand settles, the bottom layers are squashed together and slowly harden into rock. The skeleton, too, hardens and turns into rock.

*T*he different layers of rock are called strata, or beds, and new strata are slowly forming all the time.

Normally, the most recent strata are at the top, and the older rock beds at the bottom – although this is not always the case. Sometimes the strata are jumbled up because of violent earthquakes or upheavals in the earth's crust. For example, a new mountain, or even a whole range of mountains, may have been thrown up.

Sand and mud cover the body of a dead Iguanodon.

Next time you are near some cliffs, look at the cliff face and see if you can spot the different strata. Try and work out if there are any breaks in the layers.

Cliff faces are also good places to look for fossils. The rocks are always crumbling away, leaving freshly exposed areas to look at. Each stratum contains its own kinds of fossil, and all the fossils in that stratum will be much the same age.

Scientists have worked out the approximate ages of all the rocks we know about, and by studying the fossils in the various strata, have been able to build up a picture of life through the ages. All known dinosaur fossils have been found in rocks of the Mesozoic Era, the 'Age of Middle Life'. The earliest dinosaur fossil dates from about 205 million years ago, and the most recent from about 65 million years ago.

Scientists have become very good at digging up dinosaur fossils and fitting them together into skeletons. If they are very lucky, they may find a complete, or nearly complete skeleton. But even if they discover

The skeleton of an Iguanodon.

Diplodocus (double beam) lived about 130 million years ago, from the late Jurassic Period on. Although it could measure 27 metres in length, and maybe more, it had a very slender neck and tail and weighed surprisingly little. Once, it was thought that Diplodocus spent most of its time in the water, but now it is believed it may have lived among trees, feeding on the topmost twigs. It lived in groups, with the youngsters kept in the middle for safety.

only a few bones, they can often find out a lot about that animal, and how it lived. By studying a dinosaur's teeth, for example, and comparing them with the teeth of living animals, scientists can make good guesses at what sort of food it ate; by studying a dinosaur's leg and foot bones, they can work out how it walked and moved. In this way a clear, if somewhat incomplete, picture has been built up of a wide range of dinosaurs.

How dinosaurs got their names

*F*or centuries, people have occasionally dug up, or found, huge old bones, and until fairly recently, no-one knew what they were. Some people said they were the bones of giant people who lived a long time ago. But one spring day in 1822, something happened which was to prove that this, and every other theory was wrong.

A young country doctor, Dr Gideon Mantell, left his surgery in the Sussex town of Lewes to visit a patient who lived near Horsham. Because it was such a lovely day, Mrs Mantell decided to go too, and while her husband attended to his patient, she took a stroll along a nearby lane. Suddenly,

In 1676, this knee end of a dinosaur's thigh-bone was thought to have come from a human giant.

among a pile of stones left ready for some road repairs, she spotted some large fossil teeth. She picked them up and took them with her to show her husband, who was a keen collector of fossils and had written many books and papers on the subject.

As soon as Dr Mantell saw the teeth, he became very excited. Quickly, he found out where the roadstone had come from and set off for the quarry, near Cuckfield. Here he found some other fossil relics, although not a complete skeleton.

Dr Mantell correctly identified the rocks in which he had found the fossils as belonging to the Cretaceous Period. The teeth, he said, had come from a giant plant-eating reptile. But other scientists at the time did not believe him. They thought the teeth were mammal teeth; Dr Mantell had obviously been mistaken about the age of the rocks. Both sides argued a lot about it!

But Dr Mantell felt sure that he was right, and noticing that the teeth were very like those of the Common Iguana lizard of Central America, although much larger in size, he decided to call his discovery

An Iguana lizard from Central America.

Triceratops (three-horned face) was one of the last dinosaurs to survive, living for about 10 million years until the end of the Cretaceous Period, 65 million years ago. Up to 9 metres long, nearly one third of its length was an enormous bony head, with horns up to 1 metre long. It is thought to have roamed in herds, quiet and inoffensive unless attacked. It probably ate the leaves of primitive palm trees, slicing them off with its beak, and chewing them up with strong grinding teeth in very powerful jaws.

History Museum in London) proposed that all these giant reptiles should together be named dinosaurs (terrible lizards). The proposal was accepted, and this imaginative name has been used ever since.

*T*owards the end of the nineteenth century, dinosaur fever hit America. Two rival scientists – Edward Drinker Cope and Othniel Charles Marsh – each set out to find and name more dinosaurs than the other. Armed to the teeth, their separate parties travelled all over the American West, fighting off Indians, wild animals and, occasionally, each other. Between them they discovered the remains of 136 different kinds of dinosaur, nearly all of which were named according to the same system used by Dr Mantell. This system (which is still used today) involves using classical Greek or Latin names to classify animals and plants. In this way, scientists all over the world can understand what the names mean, even if they speak different languages.

*D*inosaurs have never been easy to find – although one important discovery was recently made in Surrey in south-east England. Even so, you should keep your

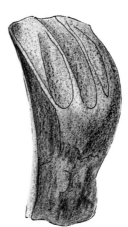

Iguanodon teeth found by Mary Ann Mantell. (Actual size.)

Brachiosaurus (arm lizard) was one of the biggest dinosaurs of all. It was up to 27 metres in length, about 12 metres tall, and weighed perhaps as much as 77 tonnes. It was built like a huge giraffe, with high shoulders, and a very long neck. Some people think it may have had a trunk, because of the shape of its skull. It ate leaves from high branches, and lived in the Late Jurassic Period.

eyes open. Who knows, perhaps you might have a lucky find one day, just like Mary Ann Mantell in that leafy lane near Horsham.

How dinosaurs are classified

Scientists divide all known dinosaurs into two main groups, or Orders. Those in the first Order are called 'lizard-hipped', or saurischian dinosaurs, because their hips are similar in shape to those of modern lizards. Those in the second Order are called 'bird-hipped' dinosaurs, or ornithischians, because their hips resemble those of modern birds. Both Orders evolved from crocodile-like reptiles called thecodonts.

Thecodonts such as Euparkeria were four-legged hunters, but their front legs were rather short so they could not run very fast. To gain speed, they therefore reared up on their stronger hind legs, and, balancing themselves with their long tails, succeeded in outrunning their prey over short distances. For hunters, this ability was such an enormous advantage that the thecodonts gradually evolved stronger and stronger back legs. So, by the time the first proper

Euparkeria sprinting.

dinosaurs appeared, they could easily stand upright on two legs, and could walk and run with considerable agility and speed. It was this new speed and agility which made these first dinosaurs the most terrifying animals there had ever been.

*B*oth saurischians and ornithischians belonged to the larger group of reptiles called archosaurs –'ruling reptiles'. Besides thecodonts and dinosaurs, the group contained the crocodilians (which survive today as crocodiles), the pterosaurs (the 'flying reptiles' which died out at about the same time as the dinosaurs), and the archaeopterytids (whose descendants are today's birds).

Saurischian dinosaurs

*T*he saurischians thrived throughout the Age of the Dinosaurs, although towards the end of the Cretaceous Period they were outnumbered by the ornithischians. Scientists divide them into two main types: the two-legged meat-eaters called theropods 'beast feet', and the four-legged plant-eaters called sauropods 'reptile feet'. There are four saurischians among the models in this book

Saurischian (lizard hips).

Stegosaurus (roof lizard) usually walked on all fours, but may have been able to rear up on its back legs to feed on the leaves of trees. Because of its weak teeth, it ate only soft plants. There were at least four heavy spikes on its tail, which it may have swung about as a weapon. Stegosaurus could measure up to 9 metres in length.

– Brachiosaurus, Diplodocus, Tyrannosaurus, and Spinosaurus. Of these, Tyrannosaurus and Spinosaurus were meat-eaters, and the other two vegetarian.

Ornithischian dinosaurs

Ornithischians were very different from saurischians. They certainly had one great advantage of strong grinding teeth concentrated in the back of their jaws. Of the two main groups of ornithischians – ornithopods and armoured dinosaurs – only the ornithopods were bipeds. The others were four-legged – plated, horned, and armoured dinosaurs. All four kinds of bird-hipped dinosaurs were plant-eaters. You can make models of three ornithischians in this book – Stegosaurus, Iguanodon, and Triceratops. Of these, Iguanodon is the only biped.

How dinosaurs lived

Like every other animal, dinosaurs had to eat to live. Many dinosaurs were herbivores and dependent for their food on the ferns and plants which grew alongside lakes and rivers. Grass did not yet exist. Other taller

Ornithischian (bird hips).

plant-eating dinosaurs probably stood up on their hind legs, to tear off leaves from the lower branches of trees. Some of the sauropods, the tallest herbivores of all, would have browsed the topmost leaves, in the way that giraffes do today. All of them spent many hours every day just finding enough food to survive.

*T*he meat-eaters had powerful claws and fangs to attack and kill their prey. The biggest were the megalosaurids–'great lizards'. They had long claws on their hands and hind feet which they used to rip through their victims' skin and muscle, as well as big, sharp, saw-edged teeth to slice through flesh. Many carnosaurs may have relied on carcasses left by other dinosaurs. They all may have had to eat their own weight in meat every week just to survive – not easy when some weighed as much as an elephant!

*B*oth carnosaurs and herbivores were probably coloured and patterned to fit in with their surroundings. This would have helped to make them less visible to their enemies, if they were herbivores; or to lie in wait, unseen, if they were carnivores. Those living among trees were probably dappled

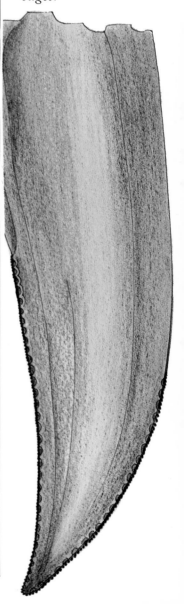

The enormous fang of a Tyrannosaurus. (Actual size.) Look at the saw-edges!

Archaeopteryx (ancient wing) was the world's first bird. It lived in the Late Jurassic Period. Although the first creature known to have feathers, it also had some features unknown in modern birds. For example, it had jaws with teeth, instead of a beak, and a long, bony tail. Few skeletons have been found, so there is still much doubt about exactly what kind of animal it was.

browns and greens; those in open spaces probably had bold patterning to disguise the shapes of their bodies.

*W*hen mating time drew near, competing males probably fought each other for the available females. They may simply have put on threatening displays, or banged heads, or hit out with their feet or tails. Once the victor had been decided, he would mate with the female, and some time later she would lay her eggs.

Some dinosaurs just buried their eggs in the sand or covered them with leaves until the warmth of the sun caused them to hatch. Other kinds apparently scooped nests out of the mud. Perhaps they even kept the eggs warm by sitting on them, a bit like a very large hen!

When the eggs hatched, some dinosaur mothers may even have brought food for their young. A few species, perhaps, shared the task of looking after the hatchlings between both mother and father. Young dinosaurs probably grew very quickly, and soon became independent of their parents.

Mating displays.

Where did the dinosaurs come from?

*W*e have already said that the dinosaurs evolved from thecodont ancestors. But where did they come from?

The story begins millions and millions of years ago, when the earth was just a swirling hot mass, circling the star we call the sun. There were no people or other animals, and no plants or trees – in fact, there was no life at all.

But then the earth cooled, and became almost completely covered with water. The sun shone, and the action of the light on chemicals in the water led to the formation of proteins. As proteins are present in all foods, their appearance meant that it was now possible for plants (and later, animals) to live and develop.

*N*obody knows quite how, but about 3,500 million years ago, tiny jelly-like blobs, the first living cells, came into existence.

These cells grew and divided, over and over again. Gradually, some of them evolved

A baby Triceratops scrabbles its way out of its shell.

Spinosaurus (thorn lizard) is easily identified by the skin sail on its back, held up by spines almost 2 metres long. It is thought that the sail helped it to warm up or cool down more quickly, by turning to catch the sun or avoid it. Unlike most meat-eaters, it had straight teeth. It was up to 12 metres long, and lived during the Late Cretaceous Period.

into the first green plants.

Plants are very important, because they give off oxygen (which allows animals to breathe) and they are the most valuable source of food. So other living creatures were now able to develop.

*E*ven so, it took millions of years before the first multi-celled animals appeared. At the beginning came simple worms and jellyfish, and other creatures without backbones (invertebrates). They were followed by sea animals which protected themselves with shells, as do crabs and oysters. Then came the first vertebrate fish, with skeletons on the insides of their bodies, and they, in turn, were followed by others with lungs and bony fins. These fish used their lungs to breathe out of the water, and their fins to haul themselves across the rocks from one pool to another, in search of food. Eventually, they became able to live almost their entire lives on the land, returning to the water only to lay their eggs. The scientific name for animals who live like this is amphibians.

Meanwhile, on the land, enormous

A lungfish clambers over the rocks, in search of food.

swamp forests had taken root and developed. There were giant 35-metre high club mosses and 10-metre tall plants called horse-tails, and the undergrowth was composed of masses of different kinds of fern. Conditions like these exactly suited the amphibians as they had plenty of food, and lots of safe hiding places in which to live and reproduce.

Then, about 290 million years ago, the amphibians gave rise to a new kind of animal – the reptiles, which were the very first animals designed to live entirely on dry land. Unlike the amphibians, which had to return to the water to lay their eggs, the reptiles laid eggs with a tough, leathery outside layer, or shell, which stopped them from drying out. This meant that for the first time, these animals did not even have to live close to water.

Slowly the reptiles branched out into separate groups. At first, they were quite small, and looked like rather thick-set lizards of today. They were hunters, and lived by catching other small animals, and also insects, of which there were now quite a few different varieties.

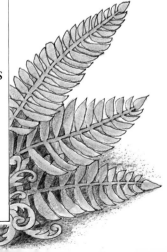

Pteranodon (toothless wing) is often mistaken for a dinosaur, although it is really a pterosaur. It lived in the Late Cretaceous Period. With a wing-span of 7 metres or more, it was one of the largest flying animals there has ever been. It weighed about the same as a large turkey, but could not fold its wings completely, as birds or bats do, so it must have been very clumsy on the ground. Perhaps it spent most of its time in the air, just as some sea-birds do now. It probably lived on fish, swooping low over the water to scoop them up in its long beak.

Later on, the reptile family included many different groups, which differed markedly in shape, size, and habits. Some, for example, like the turtles, even returned to the sea to live. They were then forced to come back to the land to lay their eggs, rather like amphibians in reverse. Other marine reptiles produced live young.

*T*he important land-living group, with which we are concerned, is called the archosaurs, and it was in this group that the thecodonts developed, and from them, the dinosaurs.

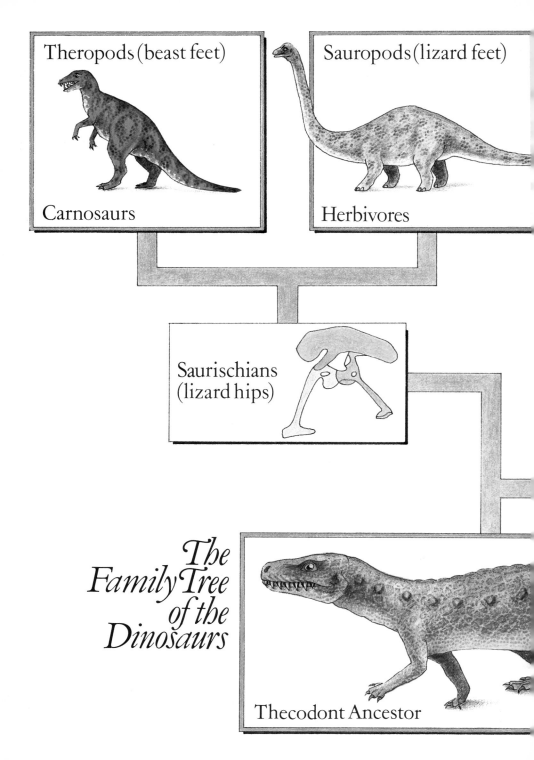

Theropods (beast feet)

Carnosaurs

Sauropods (lizard feet)

Herbivores

Saurischians
(lizard hips)

The Family Tree of the Dinosaurs

Thecodont Ancestor

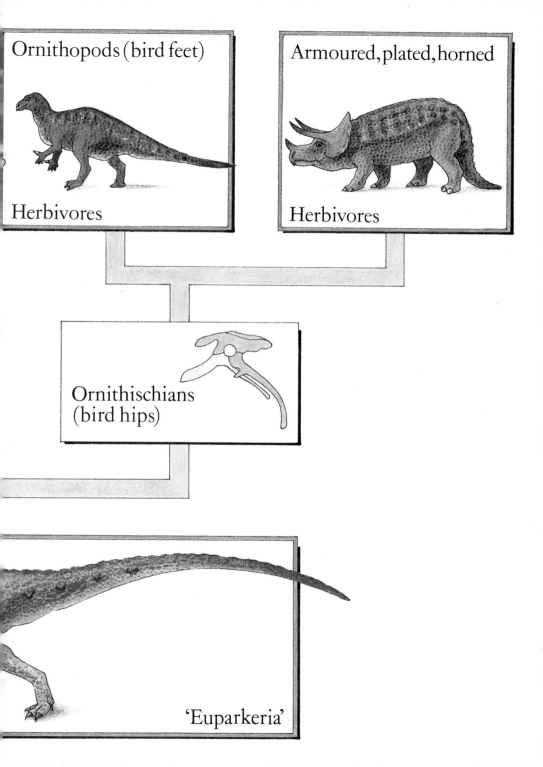

Ornithopods (bird feet)

Herbivores

Armoured, plated, horned

Herbivores

Ornithischians
(bird hips)

'Euparkeria'

Dinosaurs and you

When the dinosaurs finally died out 65 million years ago, some of their relatives lived on. For instance, Archaeopteryx (ancient wing) is generally agreed to have been the first bird even though its skeleton looks very like some of the smaller dinosaurs of the time. Some people even say that we ought to call birds 'dinosaurs', and not birds at all.

Whatever the truth about birds, the vast majority of reptiles did become extinct, and the 'Age of Dinosaurs' gave way to the 'Age of Mammals'. Like the reptiles before them, the mammals thrived and prospered. They branched out into a huge variety of animals, which, although they were all closely related by their warm blood, and giving birth to live young which they suckled with mother's milk, nonetheless came to look very different from each other. The first human-like creatures appeared about 4 million years ago – although it took another 3¼ million years before they even began to look anything like you and me.

Could this little robin really be a dinosaur?

We seem to be a very long way from dinosaurs. Yet if, as some scientists say, life has appeared on this planet only once, we are much closer than we might think. If all living things come from those original blob-like living cells, dinosaurs were in fact very distant relatives of ours!

To make this a little easier to understand, think of your own family. Everyone has, or had, two parents, four grandparents, eight great-grandparents, and so on. If you have aunts or uncles with children, these children are your cousins. Children of your parents' cousins are your second cousins. And so it continues all the way back to the beginning of life.

This means that not only are all humans 'cousins' of yours, but so is your pet dog, cat, or hamster, the sparrows and black-birds outside your window, the spider hanging in its web on the garden gate, the oak tree at the end of the road, and the dinosaurs who lived all that time ago.

Isn't that an extraordinary thing to think about?

The Calendar of the Rock

Aspect of the Earth	Period
Modern times	Recent
Four great Ice Ages	Pleistocene
Mountains formed. Cooler	Pliocene
Alps, Andes, Himalayas formed	Miocene
Sea covers Germany, Russia	Oligocene
Rocky Mountains formed	Eocene
	Palaeocene
Marine chalk deposits	Cretaceous
Seas invade continents	Jurassic
Continents high, seas limited	Triassic
Deserts in N. Europe Glaciers in S. Africa, Australia	Permian
Extensive swamp forests	Carboniferous (Coal)
Extensive warm shallow seas	Devonian
Shallow, salt seas. Hot, dry climate Coral as far North as Greenland	Silurian
Sea invasions. Volcanic activity	Ordovician
Inland seas cover most of N. America	Cambrian
Ceaseless change of land and sea	Pre-Cambrian
Ice Ages. Deserts. Volcanoes	
Great upheavals as earth's crust formed	

and the Family Tree of Life

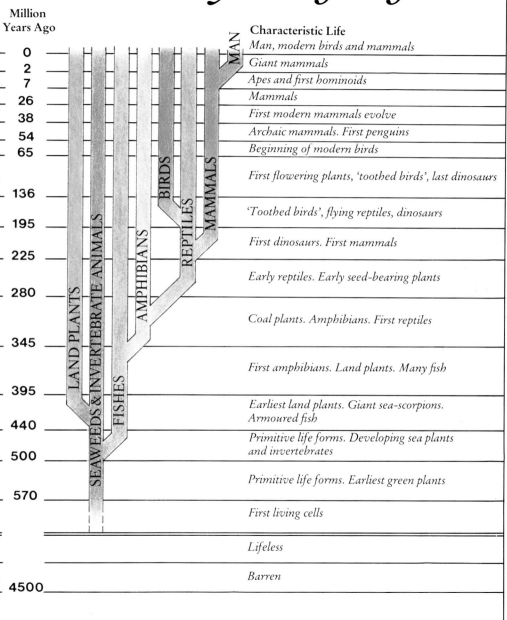

Million Years Ago	Characteristic Life
0	Man, modern birds and mammals
2	Giant mammals
7	Apes and first hominoids
26	Mammals
38	First modern mammals evolve
54	Archaic mammals. First penguins
65	Beginning of modern birds
136	First flowering plants, 'toothed birds', last dinosaurs
195	'Toothed birds', flying reptiles, dinosaurs
225	First dinosaurs. First mammals
280	Early reptiles. Early seed-bearing plants
345	Coal plants. Amphibians. First reptiles
395	First amphibians. Land plants. Many fish
440	Earliest land plants. Giant sea-scorpions. Armoured fish
500	Primitive life forms. Developing sea plants and invertebrates
570	Primitive life forms. Earliest green plants
	First living cells
	Lifeless
	Barren
4500	

Tree branches (left to right): MAN, LAND PLANTS, SEAWEEDS & INVERTEBRATE ANIMALS, AMPHIBIANS, FISHES, BIRDS, REPTILES, MAMMALS